WHAT THEY NEVER TOLD YOU ABOUT MORNING PRAYERS

BY

BISHOP OCHEI INNOCENT

"Be sober, be vigilant; because your adversary the devil, as a roaring lion, walketh about, seeking whom he may devour:"

1 Peter 5:8

DEDICATION

THIS BOOK IS DEDICATED TO INQUISITIVE CHRISTIAN YOUTHS WHO WONDER WHY WE ARE SO DEDICATED TO DAILY MORNING PRAYERS, ESPECIALLY WHEN THE COLDS ARE HERE AND MEN SHOULD STILL BE SNORING IN BED.

Contents

PREAMBLE

The Psalmist says that he will arise early in the morning and praise the Lord. There are many good reasons why that should be so. Surely, one good time to praise the Lord is early in the morning. In this little book, I have given you some untold reasons why we should start each day with prayers and praises.

Make no mistake about this: We are expected to praise God all the time and with all our breath for He is our Creator and Maker! Without him, we are nothing. It is by His mercies that we are not consumed! For these and other reasons, there is no excuse for not praising Him in season and out of season!

There are many reasons why we should learn to praise the Lord very early in the morning. Permit me to list just a few.

They say in my village that truth does not need a long rope.

The problem we have had in Christianity is that many parents take basic Christian values for granted. So they do not bother to explain these things to the younger ones. On the part of the youths, they have so many things competing for attention. It is not their fault that they live in this age of information glut.

So when we fail to explain and think that they will figure it out, we raise a generation who feel that we just did things because our parents did them and not because they are necessary and required. Youths must know that we do not just do things as routine but that God requires those who seek Him to seek him diligently so that He can be found!

FIRST, LET ME TELL YOU WHAT TOOK MRS. MICHAEL TO JAIL

I have a good reason for this story. It is about the typical housewife.

This woman loved her sleep. She was much used to slumber. I repeat for emphasis: She was not sleeping! Slumbering is the word. Every night she would sleep off like somebody who took sleeping drugs. She would sleep like a log. Even if you carry her down from the bed she will not know. Somebody once said that Mrs. Michael, for that was her name, can go to sleep in a smelter's shop!

She grew up with it and carried it into her marriage. Her husband discovered this right from the first day of their marriage. After a time of trying to correct and nag her out of the habit, her husband adjusted to the fact.

Unfortunately the husband was a drunkard. A night clubber par excellence! The only thing he lived for, apart from his doting wife, was his bottle.

 The man was always sneaking out in the night as the woman slept. He had the custom of sneaking out to brothels and meeting with prostitutes and different types of people. He was doing this regularly for a time.

An African proverb says that anybody who frequents a latrine will meet with different types of flies. One day Mr. Michael met and became friendly with some crooked young men. They began with the sharing of a bottle or two together before graduating into crime.

So Mr. Michael no longer went out just to drink but got involved in crime. Most of the crimes were things the man would never touch, if sober.

All this while, the wife believed that the husband was a dove. She never imagined that her husband could hit a fly not to talk of taking another person's property. But the group he moved with was a band of drug addicts and to sustain their evil culture they began to steal and with time they began to kill in order to steal.

They say every day is for the thief but one day is for the owner of the house. Sooner than later that proverbial day of the owner of the house came. These thieves were caught and the woman's husband was among them.

Soon as she heard the news she ran to the police station. There, she noisily quarreled with every officer she could find. She swore by all she knew that her husband was an honest man who never went out of the house one day. She even went as far as swearing an oath. She also testified in court that her husband never went out one day.

But her husband knew that he went out every night. The man also knew that the wife never knew that he was going out at night. He wanted to stop his wife from bearing false witness even in court but two things held him back. One, he could not counter the false claim of those brigands he was moving with. He feared what they would do to him when they came out of jail. Two, he did not want to go to jail. He wanted his own freedom so much. He wrongly believed that his wife's false testimony would free him.

Of course he was wrong. Unknown to him the last place the husband and his group went to steal t had closed circuit television: all of them and their activities were recorded on camera. It was only when she saw the video pictures and as her husband confessed his sins that the woman was shocked to the bone marrow.

Another African adage says that it is only the child you are carrying in your stomach you can vouch for but even the toddler you have on your back you cannot vouch for. This is so because you do not know if after you have passed a hawker on the street, the child stretched his hand and took something from the trader's tray.

Naturally, Justice must take its course. So as the husband and his gang were sentenced, the woman too got her date in jail for perjury.

Needless to say, the home was ruined beyond measure. Yes, the husband had an alcohol problem. He always had a lingering need for alcohol and began by sneaking to the fridge to help him while madam was snoring. From that he graduated to going out while she was snoring.

I am not out to heap all the blames on madam! Far from it!

Rather I blame the fact that she loves to slumber.

CHAPTER TWO

WHY HAVE I TAKEN PAINS TO NARRATE THIS STORY?

A lot of things happen in the night. There are many birds and other animals that sleep during the day only to wake up at night. They move up and down perhaps fending for their families.

So too are there many evil persons and spirits that work purely at night. Many but certainly not all, wreck evil in the night while honest men sleep! Witches and wizards for instance, meet in their coven mainly at night. When they meet in their coven they evoke names of the people that they intend to victimize amongst other things that they do. Ritual killers, magicians and other satanic groups ply their trades mainly at night!

Most of their victims prey because when a person is sleeping it becomes very difficult for that person to watch and pray in the physical realm not to talk of in the spiritual realm. They know that men are more vulnerable when they sleep than when awake. It is very rare before you see burglars and petty thieves attempting to break into a house during the day.

The Bible says that while men sleep, the wicked ones sow tares.
Most stargazers work at night. The Bible tells us of how when Jesus Christ was born some stargazer followed his star to Jerusalem. They definitely must have

been working that night which enabled them to see clearly the star and to follow it. It is not recorded anywhere that the star gave them notice of its passing bye that night.

When wicked forces monitor your star, they work evil into it. If they are not interested in harming you, they give your data to those who will. Those that saw the star of Jesus Christ went and sold the information to Herod who wanted so desperately to kill the infant whose birth had been long prophesied.

As we have criminals in the physical realm so we have criminals in the spiritual realm. Who is more criminal than Lucifer and his co-conspirators?. Their crime spree was started in the spirit real long before they fell down to the physical realm.

These criminals manipulate us from the spirit realm. As we sleep for instance, we dream and most of our dreams are manipulated by necromancers and witches using telepathy and things like that.

I have forgotten whether it is or whether it was in a movie or a book that I read something similar. In that account a person who was sleeping was magically woken up and made to do things that he would not have done in the physical. The closest to that I can think of is the misfortune of sleep walkers. They do things while they walk that they would sometimes not have done in the physical. Most times, when they wake up, they feel what they have done while sleepwalking should be undone!

Some of us easily have sex in the dream whereas in the physical we would never have done that. In the physical realm we probably have been well able to resist the temptation. Most times when we finish having such sex in the dream everything in the physical works against us. I have had a lot of people confess that to me many times.

Similarly, in the course of counseling
over the years we have had complaints
of people who became sick after eating
various kinds of foods in the dream.
There is no doubt that dreams have
positive side
but the fact remains that dreams are
easy tools in the hand of destiny
manipulators. Most of the
manipulations take place while we sleep.

People in various nations and continents
keep crying that they ate in the dream or
they had sex in the dream or somebody
was pursuing them in the dream. Some
even show marks of being beaten by
masquerades in the dream and I have
always said to them that all those things
ought to have no meaning or impact on
a Christian.

Why?

When you wake up as a child of God you
go into morning devotion and
everything will be fine with you!

It does not matter whether it is you alone doing the devotion or with the entire family. The important thing is that you do the needful every morning. Never forget that the Psalmist says in the morning I will rise and praise my God.

I am going to list for you in the next chapter, ten clear reasons why you should do this.

CHAPTER THREE

REASON TO PRAY EARLY IN THE MORNING

1. **We pray during devotions to please God**. The primary goal of prayer is to please God. Prayer is worship. When God is happy with us, He causes more lines of blessing to fall to us in pleasant places.

This is exactly what happens with our morning devotion. When we pray and praise God, He inhabits our praises and answers our supplications and intercessions.

There can therefore be no better reason
for the morning devotion, which in most
cases involves bible study and
prayers, than to please God

Let us also not forget that God himself
loves the humble and prayer is a sign of
humility.

2. **It offers us a chance to cancel all
they have done against us in the
night**. We have noted that a lot of evil
people so tense into our lives while we
sleep. We must not allow such seeds to
germinate at all.
God has given us the power to root out
and to destroy whatever the enemy had
done in the night.
This is how the bible puts it:

Jeremiah 1:10
"**See, I have this day set thee over
the nations and over the
kingdoms, to root out, and to pull
down, and to destroy, and to throw
down, to build, and to plant.**"

So we must wake up early and uproot all the evil things that they have sold into our lives.

3. It affords us the opportunity to speak to the new day and tell it what to bring and reject. In the book of Job will see God asking job whether he has spoken to the day and whether he has told the day what to bring and what not to bring

Job 38:12
"Have you ever given orders to the morning, or shown the dawn its place?"

In the same vein you are to speak to each day telling it what to bring and what not to allow. Prayer is our tool for arranging and reordering the day according to our desire and morning devotion is the perfect time because it happens right as the day is setting out.

The Bible tells me that the expectations of the righteous shall not be cut off. So why not load your expectations into the day?

4. **When we start the day with prayers, we hand that day to God**. We should have started with this very one because praying first thing in the morning is tantamount to handing over the day to God. When we hand over our life and our days to God they are in secure hands.
Our life becomes His to direct as he deems fit. And the scriptures tell us that God is the father who knowing that his son needs fish will never give him stone!

Isaiah 49:15

"Can a woman forget her sucking child, that she should not have compassion on the son of her womb? yea, they may forget, yet will I not forget thee."

Luke 11:11

"If a son shall ask bread of any of you that is a father, will he give him a stone? or if he ask a fish, will he for a fish give him a serpent?"

5. We also use morning devotion to renew our minds. The devil might have intimidated us in the night or we might have heard certain fearful sounds or noticed some activities that imposed fear in us. Devil and his agents are full of sound and fury. His purpose is to intimidate, sully up our minds and sow seeds of doubt.
For that reason, the bible urges us to renew our minds always.

Romans 12:2 [NIV]

"Do not conform to the pattern of this world, but be transformed by the renewing of your mind. Then you will be able to test and approve what God's will is--his good, pleasing and perfect will."

Coming into the presence of God with bible study, prayer, praise. and worship is like using an eraser to wipe away whatever the devil has done from our hearts.

Psalm 119:130 [KJV]

"The entrance of thy words giveth light; it giveth understanding unto the simple."

6. **When God is with you, you have peace** .When we go on our knees to pray, we enter into the presence of God and His presence is a compulsive source with peace.

<u>*2 Thessalonians 3:16*</u>

"Now may the Lord of peace himself give you peace at all times and in every way. The Lord be with all of you.'

<u>**John 14:27**</u>

27 Peace I leave with you; my peace I give you. I do not give to you as the world gives. Do not let your hearts be troubled and do not be afraid.

As we fellowship with Jesus Christ each morning we harvest peace.

It is not for nothing that Jesus Christ is referred to as the **Prince of Peace** because that is exactly what He is.

It therefore follows that when we pray every morning the Peace of God follows us wherever we are going.

7 A major advantage of morning devotion is that the children must have rested. They must have slept over the night and with a dash of water to their faces in the morning. They will be more amenable to praying with their parents than otherwise.

The same thing goes for the parents. Having rested; we are more likely to concentrate on the prayer points and the teachings of the early morning devotion than any other time.

8. **It also provides parents with another opportunity to share the scriptures with the children.**
We must seize every chance that comes our way to equip our children with the word of God.
The Bible says go to the ants and learn wisdom. We must go to companies like Coca-Cola and learn wisdom.

What do I mean by this?

Despite the fact that Coca-Cola is a household name, they are still advertising all over the Earth and per second per second. They have so advertised their brand that sometimes when we need soft drinks and we get to the supermarket, we just instinctively say "give us Coca-Cola".

Such happens because we have internalized the message of the advert.

In the same vein we must not be tired of sharing the scriptures with our children. Deuteronomy 6:6 says that we should speak and teach the word to the children when we sleep, when we work, when we go on the road and so on and so forth.

Deuteronomy 6:6-7

6 These commandments that I give you today are to be on your hearts. 7 Impress them on your children. Talk about them when you sit at home and when you walk along the road, when you lie down and when you get up."

The book of Proverbs also tells us that we should train up a child in the way we want him to go and when he grows up he will never depart from it.

Some of us parents are too anxious to rush off the child to secular schools where they are loaded with calculations and formulas but very little of God. I am not saying children should be withdrawn from schools. I am not **_Boko Haram_** Ryder I am saying that we should start early to fill our children with the word of God.

8. **Early morning devotion induces discipline.** It requires rising up early in the morning. For that to happen the children must be disciplined just like the parents.

So on the physical side and from a family perspective, morning devotion disciplines the children in terms of rising up early.

Once they imbibe this culture, it becomes a part of them and will benefit them later in life.

9. It also provides us with another opportunity to counsel the children generally about things of life. It has been said that what information teenagers do not get from their parents or teachers are happily supplied by their peers and what they are told may be a wrong version of the truth.

Morning devotion, no matter how brief, also affords us a few minutes to hear from the children. Counseling after all, is a form of communication and communication is exchange of information between two or more parties. The parents do not just talk but allow the children to lead at times, in order to know what prayer points are important from the children's perspective.

10. **For us as adults it is another opportunity to search the**

scriptures. We must not be too busy for this. Our business or jobs must not be so consuming that we do not have time for the family and God. remember always that God gave us twenty-four hours each day and the tithe of it is two hours-forty minutes! So little belongs to God!

 To teach the family and teach them right, we must first learn ourselves. Those who must lead must first be led. We as family heads and leaders must have a few minutes with God before appearing before the family. We are pastors to the family and no trained pastor goes to minister to the congregation without first studying to show himself approved.

2 Timothy 2:15

Study to shew thyself approved unto God, a workman that needeth not to be ashamed, rightly dividing the word of truth."

As a matter of fact, more reasons for morning devotion can be found. However I picked these few for brevity. The essence of an essay does not lie with the verbiage. Rather in the main points.

As good as morning devotion is to Christian living, many are not able to have it for various reasons. Knowing these reasons will enable us to be wary and not allow ourselves to be taken by them.

In the very next chapter, I shall be highlighting key issues that stop many from starting the day with quality time with God!

CHAPTER FOUR

HINDRANCES TO EARLY MORNING PRAYERS

"Watch and pray so that you will not fall into temptation. The spirit is willing, but the flesh is weak."

Mathew 26:41

There are many reasons why people do not pay attention to morning prayers. Let me, as promised at the end of the last chapter, just mention a few so that we can be conscious of them. These are mainly mundane excuses. We must not allow secular and material things to hinder us from approaching God first thing in the morning.

1. The first thing that comes to mind is the love of sleep love of sleep. Many of us like to sleep more than necessary. I am told that an adult needs only eight [8] hours a day. Unfortunately, many adults sleep for as much as eighteen hours a day!

It is children that sleep for hours on end. God is expecting an adult to stay awake and be watchful.

The Bible also says that we should do all things in moderation and that includes sleeping.

Philippians 4:5

 "Let your moderation be known unto all men. The Lord [is] at hand"

We must not also forget that too much sleep can lead to poverty. The Bible says a little sleep and a little slumber and poverty will come upon you like a thief. My advice is that we should sleep early and wake up early. Right from the cradle our parents sang to us that we must go to bed early and rise.

In **Psalm 31** we see the mother of Lemuel as she rises up early in the morning, considers a field and goes out to buy it. The same scripture tells us how the woman gets up so early to go out and earn a living.
We must know when to sleep and when to wake up.

2. Another major hindrance to early Morning Prayer is constant quarrels between husband and wife. Some couples quarrel so late into the night and for them to come together to pray in the morning becomes a problem.

In some cases they are not able to
forgive one another. Therefore
bitterness thrives in their hearts. As a
result they are not able to pray at all.
They are not even able to come together
to kneel down before the Lord because
just like Adam and Eve after they ate the
forbidden fruit they become ashamed of
appearing before the Lord and so they
are not able to pray.

The Bible strongly admonishes us to
pray in season and out of season. We are
expected to pray first thing in the
morning when we go on the road, when
we eat, when we are in the office and
even as we return to the house.

We have to pray without ceasing and
early morning is a good time to pray
because we have rested and therefore
bubbling with energy unlike night time
when we will be tired and sleepy.

1 Thessalonians 5:16-18 [ESV]

*16 **Rejoice always, 17 pray without ceasing, 18 give thanks in all circumstances; for this is the will of God in Christ Jesus for you.***

Morning devotion is another opportunity to keep the injunction to pray without ceasing.

3. **Another hindrance to early Morning Prayer is urban life.** Those of us who live in the cities have a big challenge.
That major challenge that we have is this: we wake up early to look for transportation that will take us to distant places where we work. We have to go out and earn our living but sometimes to get vehicles is herculean.

The situation is so terrible in some countries to the extent that fathers wake up much too early as I can say. This is to the extent that they go out even before their children wake up in the morning.

Unfortunately they return at a time when their children have slept. The result of this is that some of the parents and their children do not know each other.

How can such a parent find time to pray with the family every morning?

Well, no matter what happens, we must make out time to pray. Such a person needs more prayer than any other person because he or she needs God to give him a better job that allows time for prayer and the family.
We must all remember that unless the Lord says yes, we are wasting out time.

Psalm 127:2

"In vain you rise early and stay up late, toiling for food to eat-- for he grants sleep to those he loves."

Should we not rather pray for the undying love of God?

4. **Another hindering factor is when the family goes to bed very late.** This happens for a number of reasons. The main one I can think about is when the family does not cook on time. So even as they are having dinner everybody is sleeping off.

 It should not be so. Families must learn to cook early and eat. It is better to plan things out so that the family can have dinner early and can have the family devotion before sleeping and waking up also to pray in the morning.

We must remember that the bible says that for everything under the sun, there is a time.

5 **A lot of people today are suffering from telephone addiction.** We press our phones from morning to night. We are so much to be found with our phones that one now wonders how people were coping when there were no mobile phones.

We have become so addicted with our phones that we have no time for sleep and none for our God it appears. How I wish we can all recharge our souls with the Word of God the way we charge our phones.

We are so used to pressing the phones that even when it is time for family devotion some of us are asking that the prayers be deferred just because we are pressing our phones.

For the same sake of pressing the phones and browsing the internet many do not have time for going to sleep on time. So they end up going to bed so late that they do not wake up early to pray.

May God have mercy on us all!

My advice again is have time for everything and adhere strictly to your time schedule for everything.

Ecclesiastes 3:1-8

A Time for Everything

3 There is a time for everything,

and a season for every activity under the heavens:

2 a time to be born and a time to die,

a time to plant and a time to uproot,

3 a time to kill and a time to heal,

a time to tear down and a time to build,

4 a time to weep and a time to laugh,

a time to mourn and a time to dance,

5 a time to scatter stones and a time to gather them,

a time to embrace and a time to refrain from embracing,

6 a time to search and a time to give up,

a time to keep and a time to throw away,

7 a time to tear and a time to mend,

a time to be silent and a time to speak,

8 a time to love and a time to hate,

a time for war and a time for peace."

6. **Some of us are simply lazy**. Once we are in bed we find it difficult to get up for no other reason than laziness. The Bible says that some of us are so afflicted with laziness that we find it difficult even to lift our hand, full of food, into his own mouth.

Proverbs 19:24

***"The sluggard buries his hand in the dish,
But will not even bring it back to his mouth."***

Source: https://bible.knowing-jesus.com/topics/Sluggards

Some of us are so lazy that we see prayer as big work and therefore shy away from it. Not just early Morning Prayer but prayer as a whole we see as a big walk.

7. We read novels far into the night.

Again, there is time for everything under the sun, everything under the sun. We must stop reading far into the night. Some of us enjoy novels so much that we do not know that time has gone.

Whatever our reason, we cannot be tired of telling you that there is time for everything and that includes a time to stop reading and go to bed so as to wake up early in the morning and pray.

8. **Mention must also be specifically made of watching late movies.** This also contributes to our not being able to wake up early in the morning and pray.

9. **Putting the children in distant schools** also contributes to this anomaly. The further your children's schools are from your home, the more the need for you to wake up early in the morning and prepare for them so that they will not be late to school.

This in turn affects your ability to have your early morning prayers since you have to start early to prepare for them. This can be avoided.

The Bible says that wisdom profits and that wisdom is profitable to direct.

Ecclesiastes 10:10

"If the iron be blunt, and he do not whet the edge, then must he put to more strength: but wisdom is profitable to direct."

 Wisdom demands that we look for schools near our homes and put our children.

10. **Another factor that may not be ignored is our political meetings.** This category of meetings fall into what we can also classify as nocturnal meetings.

Some high-profile persons are in the habit of holding meetings far too late into the night and this makes it extremely difficult for them to wake up early and pray.

Whatever takes your attention to the extent that you cannot find time to pray

and worship God as you should has
become an idol to you.

1 John 5:21 -

*"Little children, keep yourselves
from idols. Amen.*

Psalms 16:4 -

*"Their sorrows shall be
multiplied [that] hasten [after]
another [god]: their drink
offerings of blood will I not offer,
nor take up their names into my
lips."*

King David of Israel was a king and
politician. He ruled a difficult people
and conquered many nations.

Yet, there was hardly any major decision
he took without first consulting God. He
even had time to listen to Nathan
though it be a rebuke.

Do not be too busy with politics as to not
have time for God every morning.

CHAPTER FIVE

MORE SCRIPTURES THAT SUPPORT MORNING PRAYERS

<u>Proverbs 8:17</u> -

I love them that love me; and those that seek me early shall find me

.

<u>Psalms 57:8</u> -

Awake up, my glory; awake, psaltery and harp: I [myself] will awake early.

Mark 1:35 -

And in the morning, rising up a great while before day, he went out, and departed into a solitary place, and there prayed.

Psalms 5:3 -

My voice shalt thou hear in the morning, O LORD; in the morning will I direct [my prayer] unto thee, and will look up.

KINDLY SEE IF YOU CAN GIVE ANSWERS TO THESE QUESTIONS

1. WHY DO YOU THINK MORNING PRAYERS ARE VERY IMPORTANT?
2. GIVE THREE REASONS WHY SOME FAMILIES AVOID MORNING DEVOTION?
3. MENTION THREE THINGS THAT SHOULD BE IN MORNING DEVOTION.
4. DO THE CHILDREN HAVE ANY INPUT IN THE MORNING DEVOTION?
5. MENTION THREE SCRIPTURES THAT SUPPORT MORNING DEVOTION?

6. WHY SHOULD THERE BE TIME FOR EVERYTHING?

7. WHAT HAPPENS WHEN SPOUSES QUARREL OVERNIGHT?

8. HOW CAN MORNING DEVOTION HELP THE CHILDREN?

9. AS A YOUTH, WHAT IS YOUR OPINION OF MORNING DEVOTION?

10. HOW DOES READING FAR INTO THE NIGHT OR WATCHING LATE MOVIES AFFECT FAMILY DAILY DEVOTIONS?

THANKS FOR READING THROUGH.

SHOULD YOU HAVE A NEED FOR PRAYERS, PLEASE EMAIL ME AT;
newochei@gmail.com

I ALSO ENCOURAGE YOU TO REACH ME WITH SUGGESTIONS YOU HAVE FOR THE IMPROVEMENT OF THIS BOOK IN THE NEXT EDITION.YOU CAN ALSO LEAVE AN HONEST REVIEW ON AMAZON.

ONCE MORE I THANK YOU FOR CHOOSING TO READ THIS BOOK AND I PRAY THAT ONE WORD REMAINS IN YOU LIFE FROM THIS LITTLE BOOK.

OTHER BOOKS BY THE SAME AUTHOR

1. HOW TO DEAL RUTHLESSLY WITH THE SPIRIT OF CONSPIRACY.
2. HOW TO DEAL RUTHLESSLY WITH SIN.
3. HOW TO DEAL RUTHLESSLY WITH USE AND DUMP SPIRIT.
4. HOW TO DEAL RUTHLESSLY WITH HATRED AND RACISM.
5. SO YOU CALL YOURSELF A PASTOR?
6. SO YOU CALL YOURSELF A MANAGER?
7. SO YOU CALL YOURSELF A HUSBAND?

ABOUT THE AUTHOR

BISHOP OCHEI INNNOCENT, 64, IS THE PRESIDENT OF NEW DIMENSION SEMINARIES INTERNATIONAL.

HE IS A MEMBER OF THE INTERNATIONAL FELLOWSHIP OF THE CHRISTIAN CRISIS CENTERS, USA.

HE IS MARRIED TO LIZZY AND THEY ARE BLESSED WITH FOUR GOD FEARING CHILDREN

HE HAS BEEN IN MINISTRY FOR THREE DECADES AND IT HAS BEEN NOTHING BUT A FAITH WALK.

ABOUT THE BOOK

THE HUSTLE AND BUSTLE OF LIFE SEEM TO HAVE EATEN AWAY OUR FAMILY MORNING DEVOTIONS. WHERE IT STILL EXISTS, IT COMES ONCE A WHILE.

MANY OF OUR CHILDREN HAVE LOST INTEREST. THEY ARE NOT TOTALLY TO BLAME BECAUSE MANY DO NOT KNOW WHY SUCH EARLY MORNING PRAYERS ARE IMPORTANT!

THIS BOOK DETAILS THE IMPORTANCE OF MORNING FAMILY DEVOTIONS AND HIGHLIGHTS THE HINDRANCES SO THAT WE CAN BE MORE WARY.

IT IS AN IDEAL GIFT TO THE
YOUTH OF TODAY WHO NEEDS
TO KNOW WHY WE DO CERTAIN
THINGS AND NOT JUST BE
FORCED TO ACCEPT WHAT THEY
DO NOT UNDERSTAND.

NOTES

NOTES

NOTES

NOTES

www.ingramcontent.com/pod-product-compliance
Lightning Source LLC
Chambersburg PA
CBHW052129150726
48002CB00006B/2539